Corn Crops

by Grace Hansen

Abdo Kids Jumbo is an Imprint of Abdo Kids
abdobooks.com

abdobooks.com

Published by Abdo Kids, a division of ABDO, P.O. Box 398166, Minneapolis, Minnesota 55439.
Copyright © 2024 by Abdo Consulting Group, Inc. International copyrights reserved in all countries.
No part of this book may be reproduced in any form without written permission from the publisher.
Abdo Kids Jumbo™ is a trademark and logo of Abdo Kids.

Printed in the United States of America, North Mankato, Minnesota.

052023

092023

THIS BOOK CONTAINS RECYCLED MATERIALS

Photo Credits: Alamy, Getty Images, Shutterstock, United States Department of Agriculture

Production Contributors: Teddy Borth, Jennie Forsberg, Grace Hansen
Design Contributors: Victoria Bates, Candice Keimig

Library of Congress Control Number: 2022946710
Publisher's Cataloging-in-Publication Data

Names: Hansen, Grace, author.

Title: Corn crops / by Grace Hansen

Description: Minneapolis, Minnesota : Abdo Kids, 2024 | Series: Agriculture in the USA! | Includes online
    resources and index.

Identifiers: ISBN 9781098266189 (lib. bdg.) | ISBN 9781098266882 (ebook) | ISBN 9781098267230
    (Read-to-me ebook)

Subjects: LCSH: Crops--Juvenile literature. | Agriculture--Juvenile literature. | Farming--Juvenile
    literature. | Field crops--Juvenile literature.

Classification: DDC 633.15--dc23

Table of Contents

Top Crop

Corn is a very important crop.

The United States is the largest

corn producer in the world!

The History of Corn

Teosinte is a wild grassy plant **native** to Mexico. Farmers began growing it around 10,000 years ago. The plant **yielded** a few kernels. By 4,500 years ago, humans had developed a plant closer to modern corn. It was grown throughout the Americas.

7

Corn Crops

Today corn is grown in all 50 states. The Midwest is the main corn-growing region. Iowa is the top corn producer.

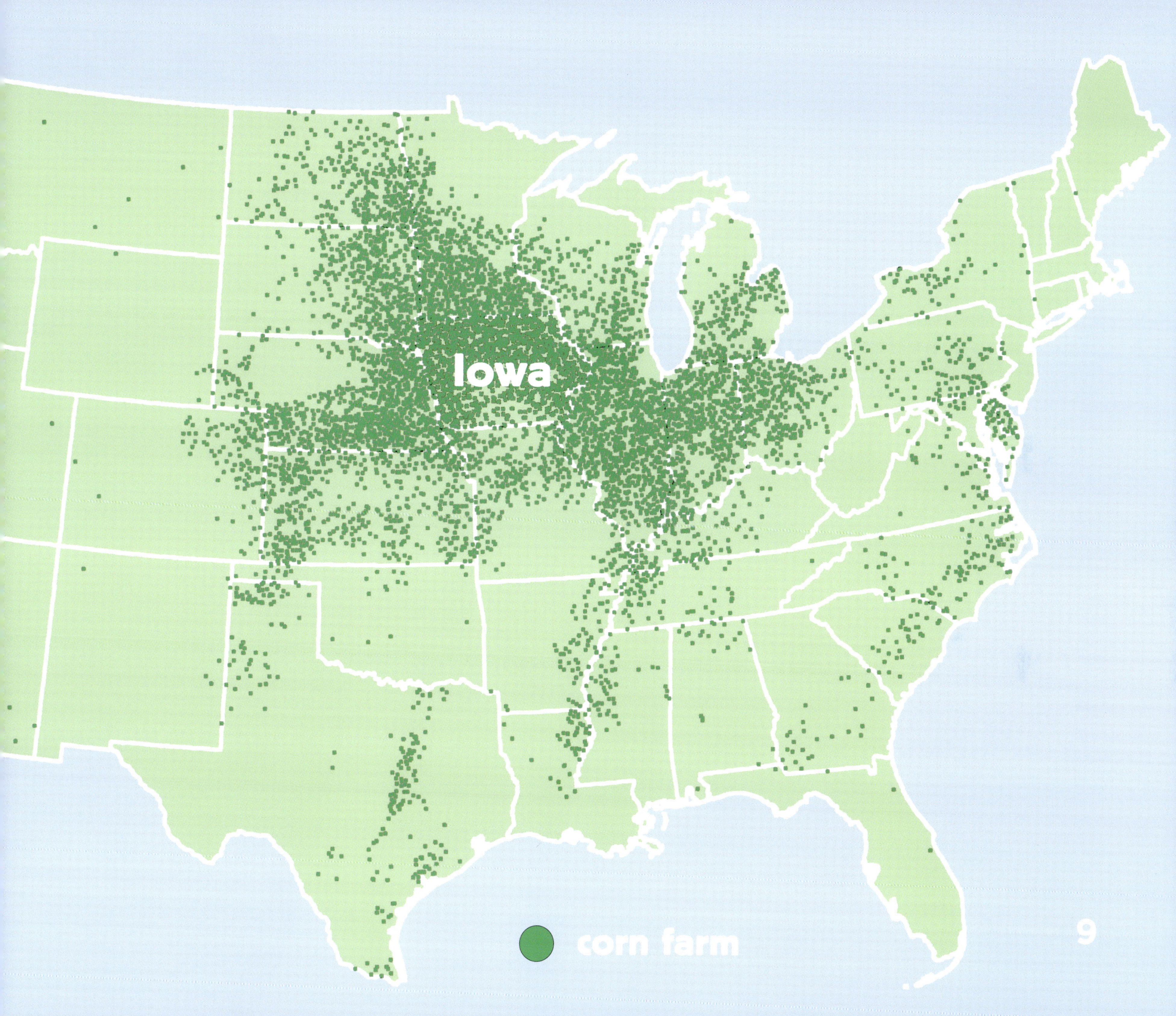
Iowa
corn farm

Most corn grown in the US is field corn. Field corn has many uses such as feeding livestock and making **ethanol**. It is also used in products such as paper, shampoo, crayons, and soda.

Sweet corn makes up just 1% of corn planted in the United States. It has plump, juicy kernels. It is meant to be eaten.

All corn grows from a single kernel. Each corn stalk grows two ears of corn. In the Midwest, farmers begin planting kernels in late April or early May. This can take about two weeks.

Seedlings can take anywhere from 1 to 3 weeks to **emerge**. This depends on soil temperature. The warmer the soil, the quicker seedlings will sprout.

Field corn is ready for harvest in late summer or early fall. It is fully ripe when it is picked. It is inspected, dried out, and stored in a grain elevator. Soon it will ship to mills for processing.

Sweet corn is **harvested** earlier in the growing process. Farmers inspect each ear in early summer. Sweet corn is then boxed, put on pallets, and kept cool. It is shipped fresh to grocery stores, canned, or frozen.

Parts of a Corn Plant

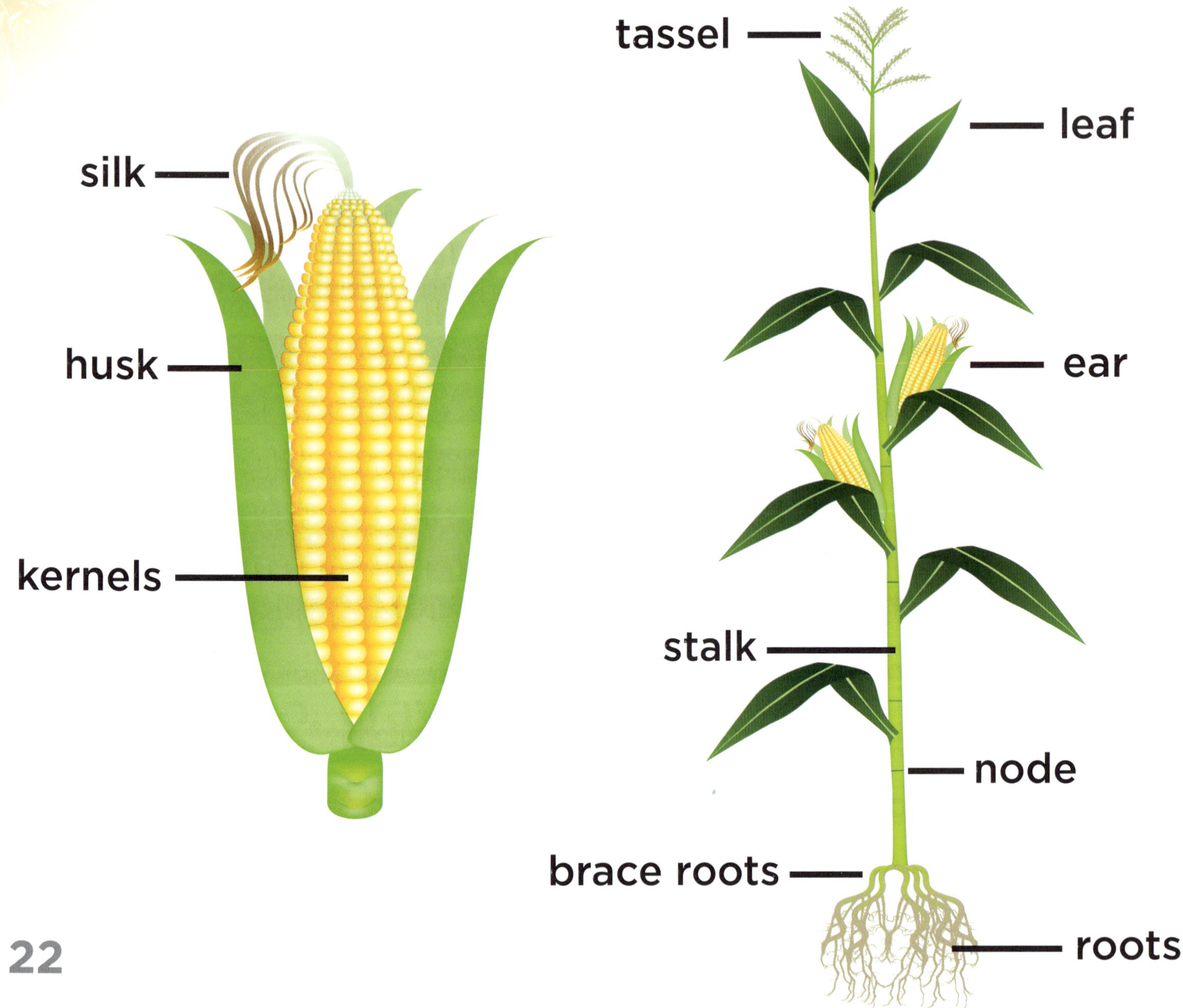

Glossary

emerge – to rise up from or come into view.

ethanol – a renewable fuel made from various plant materials. More than 98% of US gasoline contains ethanol.

harvest – the gathering of ripe crops, the crops or the amount of crops gathered, or the season in which they are gathered.

mill – a place where raw grains are crushed and ground to make flour.

native – a plant naturally found in a given place.

seedling – a young plant grown from a seed.

yield – the thing or amount produced.

Index